张文新
油画选

SELECTED OIL PAINTINGS
OF ZHANG WENXIN

河北美术出版社

张文新油画选

河 北 美 术 出 版 社 出 版
（ 石 家 庄 市 北 马 路 45 号 ）
河 北 新 华 印 刷 二 厂 印 刷
河 北 省 新 华 书 店 发 行
1988 年 9 月 第 1 版 第 1 次 印 刷
I S B N 7—5310—0211—6／J·207
定价　23元

笔巧意深　韵趣盎然

何孔德

　　近年来在美术界常见到"崛起"、"推出"之类的新词，某些理论家还认定这是一种"运动"，运动的中坚力量是一些美术"群体"。既是"群体"，又是"运动"，似乎"天然有理"了。有些人甚至提出要"肃清传统，扫除权威"，大有"破字当头、立在其中"之势。文革十年，劫后余生的我们，不免有个疑问：这是我国美术的现状？发展的趋势？还是哪几个理论家的主观臆断？

　　我不具备那种能看到将来与宇宙的慧眼，只能看到我们的时代，我们国家的现在和过去。就油画艺术而言，并非不赞成创新，不需要崛起，也不能说没有过崛起。如果认为别人一切都不行，"老子天下第一"，当然他会前无古人，后无来者，"念天地之悠悠，独怆然而泣下"了。如果对祖国的文化还有起码的了解，对西方不那么盲目崇拜的话，就不难看出我们的油画曾产生过一些高水平的作品，高水平的画家，并且有自己独特的体系，有西方无法代替的价值。

　　自吹可鄙、自卑可悲。要恰如其分地估量我们的成就与不足，要有自尊心和自信心，当代中国人并不比外国人差。我国参加国际歌剧、小提琴比赛曾得过金奖，油画就注定不如人？我不这样看，我认为中国的油画几十年来的发展，特别是建国后的成就，已形成一个艺术的高原，在高原上耸立着许多群峰。如果我说张文新的油画，就是其中一峰，我想大家是会同意的。

　　张文新早在五十年代初，就创作了《诗朗诵》、《在少年之家》等画，颇有些名气。一九五七年他为建军三十周年美展创作的《工程列车》，显露出他高超的艺术天才和生动准确的造型能力。画面上那些性格鲜明的人物，至今仍活跃在我脑际。六十年代初他创作的《间苗》，可以说是他在油画技巧上达到炉火纯青的阶段。在当时表现农民题材的油画中，《间苗》可以说是佼佼者，它之所以出众，有别于他人，是他的表现手法，构思超脱一般化，未落入"你追我赶"、"六畜兴旺"、"人寿年丰"之类的老套；更不以表现妇女的婀娜多姿来博得观众的赞赏，而是从平凡习见的劳动场面，以自然优美的生产动作，平凡中显现出不一般；他以响亮明快的色彩、贴切流畅的笔触、刻画出一派阳光，一片新绿，呈现生意盎然的景象，像一支怡美的田园诗。在张文新许多画里，表现出来的气韵、虚实、明暗、强弱变化，都饱含了丰富的韵律和节奏感。

　　十年动乱之后，许多画家对主题性创作再也不愿沾边，张文新经过坎坷经历后，大难不死，锐气尤存，不怕险、不畏难，连续创作了《巍巍太行》、《一往无前》这样史诗般的巨幅力作，气势雄浑，场面宏伟，成为美术馆和博物馆的珍品。

　　除大量主题性创作之外，还有更多的肖像画、风景写生、习作等小幅作品，均有很高的欣赏价值，给人以新的启迪。要做到构思巧，手法高，习作创作同样精采是不容易的。往往有些是想得好而表现不出来，习作笔法流畅而创作枯燥板滞；大幅作品流于粗疏，小幅作品流于空泛。张文新则不论画幅大小都能得心应手，响亮而不浮华、蕴蓄而不晦涩。潇洒细腻相兼，无炫耀技法之迹，同行从中可见其深厚功底和淳朴的艺术气质。

　　我想，这些都不是溢美之词，读者看了画集就可得以印证。

一九八七年七月于京

SKILLFUL BRUSH REVEALS MEANINGS PROFOUND FUSION OF SPIRIT AND MATTER FLOWS WITH RHYTHMIC CHARM

By He Kungde Translated by John H. Yee

In recent years one often sees such new terms as "crop ups", "turn outs". Some theorists even consider this as a "movement". At the core of this movement, are some groups of young artists of the abstract school. Being a "group" and involved in a "movement", it must then be considered as following the Nateral Principle. Some people even go so far as to suggest the need to expunge traditional oil paintings and purge their authority. Their attitude is stronly imbued wity the revolutionary philosophy that "out of the ashes, ermerge the new pheonix". After then years of Deluge (The Cultural Revolution 1965-75),we the survivors have a doubting question: Is this the present state of affairs of art in our country (China)? Is this the direction art will take in its future develop. ment? Or is it the subjective theory and interpretation of a few theorists?

I am not equipped with the wisdom or insight to see into the future or possible changes in the universe; but can only look at our own times, and the past and present of our own country (China). As for oil painting, it is not that I do not advocate the rise of new art styles, or that there isn't a need for new art styles; nor can it be said that there hasn't been any emergence of new art styles in the past. But if one takes the view that "I alone am the greatest, nothing anyone else does is any good", then naturally, like the tragic poet Chu Yuan of ancient times, he will bemoan the affairs of State and "upon the wide world stand alone and weep." But if one possesses a minimum understanding of the culture of one's motherland (China), and not worship the West so blindly, it would be none too difficult to see that among our oil paintings and oil painting artists, there has been some which are of high standards. They are artists of high caliber, with an artistic approach uniquely their own.

To boast of one's ability is base, but having an inferiority complex is regretable. What is needed is a fair and unbiased, critical estimation of our accomplishments and our short comings. There must be within us a feeling of self respect, as well as faith in ourselves; for Chinese of today are decidedly not inferior to peoples of other lands. In our natiotnal participation of various international contests, such as in music, voice, violin and many other fields, we have won many gold medals and trophies. And yet in oil paintings we do not measure up to others? I do not see it this way. I maintain that the oil paintings of China, through its continued development during the several decades, particularly its accomplishments since the establishment of the People's Republic of China in 1949, has risen to a new plateau. On this plateau stands many peaks.If l say that Zhang Wenxin's oil paintings represent one of these peaks, I believe everyone will agree.

As early as the 1950's, Zhang Wenxin had created many oil paintings, including "Youth Reciting Poetry", and "At the Youth Academic Palace". The latter having received an award from the Beijing Cultural Bureau in 1953, which earned him a good reputation. In 1957, in the art exhibit to commemorate the 30th Anniversary of the Founding of the Liberation Army (1927-57), Mr. Zhang created the "Engineers' Train" which revealed his superior talent and the ability to create life movement with breathlike accuracy. The personalities in the painting, portrayed with such distinct individuality and spirit, remains so vividly in mymind's eye, even to this day.

"Thining the Plants" which he painted in early 1963, may be said to truly reveal his high level of attainment in technique and skill in oil painting. Among the oil paintings which focused on the theme of peasant life at the time, "Thining of the Plants" may be said to be unsurpassed. What makes it stand out among others and uniquely different, is his technique in artistic expression which shows immense power of integration, bringing forth thewhole rythm of nature. Thus his works rise above the ordinary, and does not fall to the level of "Wild pursuit" or"Gathering the Full Harvest" types of feverish competition. Nor does he turn to painting beautiful maidens togain public acclaim. Instead, he focuses on the daily life of ordinary people, from the natural and beautiful aspects of daily activity, from the common life movements, he brings out the true beauty of the ordinary. For he has gone beyond looking to seeing; and he has opened our eyes to see. For in today's complex world,most of us do a lot of looking, but we see less and less. Gadgets and labels have taken over our thinking, feeling, experiencing and seeing.

Zhang Wenxin's paintings escape the ordinary, perhaps because he no longer looks at what he sees, but has become one with them, thus achieving effortless creation which comes from oneness with the Dao. Thushe is able to create, from brilliant colours and free flowing brush strokes, the armth of sunlight, a patch of green, portraying an exuberant mood, lken unto a pastoralsymphony. So we see in many of Zhang Wenxin's paintings,the revalation of the human spirit. Solid and voids, dark and light, and changes in the strong and weak, all co;ntain a rich rythm of life.

Afater ten years of the Cultural Revo;lution, many artists refused to touch "topic" painting. But Zhang Wenxin who also suffered "the slings and arrows of outrageous fortune" during this period of political struggle, was different. Escaping desth in a time of turmoil, his spirit remained unbroken. Unafraid of danger and hardship, he soon created "Towering Taihang Mountain", portraying the people's struggle during the Sino-Japanese War. Another painting "Forward" or"Yi Wang Wu Qian", was an epic-like large painting which showed the heroic human spirit in a grand and majestic setting. The painting has made it the jewel of historical and art museum collectors.

Besides creating a large quantity of topical paintings,there are even more paintings of portraits, the outdoors, and preliminary works, all of which are noteworthy and enjoyable works to see, affording the viewer a new sense of revalation and inspiration. To master the skills of translating thought to the canvas, and to develop a high technique in painting and preliminary work with the same degree of expertise, is not at all easy. Quite frequently, some painters who possess excellent ideas, are unable to express them on canvas,or else are good at prelimenary sketch work but become stuck when they are working on canvas. As a result, large paintings appear coarse andout of touch, while small ones give a feeling of being empty and no; n specific. But Zhang Wenxin's paintings, be they large or small, always turn out with high proficiency. He is brilliant without being ostenatious, mellow without being obscure and hardgoing. Broad strokes and fine details blend in harmony, and one finds no trace of high technique, but can see the subtle but definite imprint; of extensive training, and the pure and unadulterated artistic disposition of the artist.

I believe what I have said is objective and not excessive praise. At any rate, the reader, after examining his art collections, will be in a good position to survey my judgement.

间苗　1963
麻布，油彩，50×150cm
私人藏

Thinning 1963
oil on canvas，50×150cm
Private collection

巡猎　1983
麻布，油彩，73×140cm
美国私人藏

Patrol 1983
oil on canvas, 73×140cm
Private collection, U. S. A

绣新衣　　1984
麻布，油彩，
72.7×60.6cm
中国美术馆藏

Embroidering Dowry 1984
oil on canvas,
72.7×60.6cm
China Art Gallery, Beijing

春米   1984
麻布，油彩，110×59.5cm
美国私人藏

Husking Rice 1984
oil on canvas, 110×59.5cm
Private collection, U. S. A

4

温暖的火膛　1985
麻布，油彩，
65×53cm
私人藏

Warm Light 1985
oil on canvas,
65×53cm
Private collection

骑驴的女孩　1986
麻布，油彩，
65×53cm
私人藏

Gril on Donkey **198**
oil on canvas,
65×53cm
Private collection

纺线女　1986
麻布，油彩，87.5×87.5cm
私人藏

Spinning Wowan 1986
oil on canvas, 87.5×87.5cm
Private collection

耕耘　1986
麻布，油彩，67×132.5cm
私人藏

Plowing 1986
oil on canvas, 67×132.5cm
Private collection

柴扉 1986
麻布，油彩，100×70**cm**
私人藏

At the Home's Gate **1986**
oil on canvas, 100×70cm
Private collection

村戏　1986
麻布，油彩，86.5×116cm
私人藏

Village Theatric 1986
oil on canvas, 86.5×116cm
Private collection

歌　1987
，油彩，
×76.2cm
藏

g's Song 1987
n canvas,91.5×76.2cm
ate collection

渔家女　1983—86
麻布，油彩，39×63cm
私人藏

Fishman's Daughter 1983—86
oil on canvas, 39×63cm
Private collection

纳集市　1986

布，油彩，

×55cm

人藏

arket in Banna **1986**

on canvas, 65×55cm

×55cm

ivate collection

织女　1986
麻布，油彩，50×60cm
私人藏

Dai Nationalify's Weaving Woman 1986
oil on canvas, 50×60cm
Private collection

14

兰兰的早餐　1987
麻布，油彩，80×50cm
美国格林维治公司藏

Lan Lan's Braekfast 1987
oil on canvas, 80×50cm
Greenwish Workshop, U. S. A

猎　1984
麻布，油彩，50×100cm
私人藏

Hunting 1984
oil on canvas, 50×100cm
Private collection

晒场院　　1985
麻布，油彩，61×40.5cm
私人藏

Threshing Ground 1985
oil on canvas, 61×40.5cm
Private collection

小卓玛，你上哪儿去？ 1988
麻布，油彩，79×117cm
私人藏

Where Are You Going? Lettle Zhuoma
oil on canvas, 79×117cm
Private collection

女律师   1983
麻布，油彩，45.5×37cm
美国私人藏

Woman Attorney **1983**
oil on canvas, 45.5×37cm
Private collection,U. S. A

北京姑娘　　1984
纸板，油彩，51×39cm
日本私人藏

Gril from Beijing 1984
oil on paper, 51×39cm
Private collection, Japan

衣的女孩　1984

，油彩，

×37cm

私人藏

in Red Jacket 1984

n canvas, 45.5×37cm

ate collection, Japan

阿拉伯语教师　1982
麻布，油彩，41×31.8cm
埃及私人藏

Arabic Teacher 1982
oil on canvas, 41×31.8cm
Private collection, Egypt

梅地　　1985
麻布，油彩，44.5×33cm
菲律宾梅地藏

Meddy 1985
oil on canvas, 45.5×33cm
collected by Meddy, Philippines

姑娘和花　1983
纸板，油彩，32 .5×58cm
私人藏

Gril and Flowers 1983
oil on paper, 32.5×58cm
Private collection

金秋　1985
纸板，油彩，45×33cm
美国私人藏

Golden Autumn 1985
oil on paper, 45×33cm
collected by Johnny
Su, U. S. A

◁等待　1984
麻布，油彩，110×50cm
美国格林维治公司藏

Waiting　**1984**
oil on canvas, 110×50cm
Greenwish Workshop,
U.S.A

▽布衣族姑娘　1986
纸板，油彩，39×25.8cm
私人藏

Buyi Nationality Gril **198**
oil on paper, 39×25.8cr
Private collection

宾丽　1980
纸板，油彩，
34×32.6cm
日本私人藏

Binli 1980
oil on paper,
34×32.6cm
Private collection,
Japan

人体　1986
麻布，油彩，53.6×72.7cm
美国私人藏

Nude 1986
oil on canvas, 53.6×72.7cm
Private collection, U. S. A

浴后　1986
麻布，油彩，120..5×56.5×cm
私人藏

After the Bath 1986
oil on canvas, 120.5×56.5cm
private collection

江南雨　1986
纸板，油彩，
39×33cm
私人藏

Southern Drizzle 1986
oil on paper, 39×33cm
Private collecion

苏州小桥流水　1986
麻布，油彩，75×100cm
私人藏

Suzhou, River and Bridge **1986**
oil on canvas, 75×100cm
Private collection

渔舟　1984
麻布，油彩，50×60cm
日本私人藏

Fishing Boat 1984
oil on canvas, 50×60cm
Private collection, Japan

水乡　1986
纸板，油彩，35×51cm
日本私人藏

Watery Country **1986**
oil on paper, 35×51cm
Private collection, Japan

小吃店　1984
纸板，油彩，27×33cm
日本保野透藏

Snack Lunchroom 1984
oil oń paper, 27×33cm
collected by Hoku Nao, Japan

责任编辑：林日雄
装帧设计：劲　草

Responable Editor Lin Rixiong
Designed by Jin Cao

CONTENTS

目　录